夏日女孩

浩瀚◎编

厦门大学出版社 | 国家一级出版社
XIAMEN UNIVERSITY PRESS | 全国百佳图书出版单位

目　录

All You Remember

All you remember about your child being an infant is the incredible awe you felt about the precious miracle you created. You remember having plenty of time to bestow all your wisdom[①] and knowledge. You thought your child would take all of your advice and make fewer mistakes, and be much smarter than you were. You wished for your child hurry to grow up.

All you remember about your child being two is never using the restroom alone or getting to watch a movie without talking animals. You remember worrying about the bag of M&M's melting in your pocket and ruining your good dress. You wished for your child to be more independent.

All you remember about your child being seven is the carpool[②] schedule. You learned to apply makeup in two minutes and brush your teeth in the rearview mirror because the only time you had for yourself was when you were stopped at red lights. You considered painting your car yellow and posting a "taxi" sign on the lawn next to the garage door. You remember people staring at you the few times you were out of the car, because you kept flexing your foot and making acceleration noises. You wished for the day your child would learn how to drive.

All you remember about your child being ten is managing the school fund-raisers. You sold wrapping paper for paint, T-shirts for new furniture, and magazine subscriptions for shade trees in the school playground. You remember storing a hundred cases of candy bars in the garage to sell so the school band could get new uniforms, and how they melted together on an unseasonably warm spring afternoon. You wished your child would grow out of playing an instrument.

All you remember about your child being fourteen is being asked not to stop the car in front of the school in the morning. You had to drive two blocks further and unlock the doors without coming to a complete stop. You remember not getting to kiss your child goodbye or talking to him in front of his friends. You wished your child would be more mature.

All you remember about your child being eighteen is the day they were born and having all the time in the world.

And, as you walk through your quiet house, you wonder where they went and you wish your child hadn't grown up so fast.

词汇

① wisdom　智慧;学问

② carpool　合伙使用汽车

你所记得的一切

当你的孩子是个婴儿时，你所记得的，是你对自己创造出的珍贵奇迹，感到不可思议的敬畏。你记得你有大量的时间去传授你所有的智慧和知识。你认为你的孩子将会接受你所有的忠告而少犯错误，将会比孩提时代的你聪明许多。你多希望你的孩子快快长大。

孩子两岁时，你所记得的，是他从不能独自使用卫生间，从不看一部与动物无关的电影。你记得你担心那袋 M&M 巧克力糖会在你的衣兜里融化，毁了你体面的衣服。你多希望你的孩子更独立些。

孩子七岁时，你所记得的，是安排合伙用车的时间。你学会了在两分钟内化完妆，照着汽车后视镜刷牙，因为你能给自己找出的时间就只有汽车停在红灯前的那一小段。你想过把你的车子漆成黄色，并在车库门旁的草坪上立一个“出租车”的标志牌。你记得有几次你下车后，人们盯着你，因为你不断用脚踩油门加速，制造噪音。你多希望孩子有一天能学会开车。

孩子 10 岁时，你所记得的，是怎么应付学校的募捐者。你们为重新粉刷学校兜售包装纸，为购置新家具兜售 T 恤衫，为在学校操场上种植遮阳树劝人订阅各种杂志。你记得你在车库里存放了上百盒糖果等待出售，得到钱后学校的乐队就可以购置新制服，可是那些糖果竟在春天一个暖和得过头的下午全都融化在一起了。你多希望孩子长大，不再演奏什么乐器了。

孩子 14 岁时，你所记得的，是他不让你早晨把汽车停在校门口。你不得不开过两个街区，车还没停稳就赶紧打开车门。你记得没能在他的朋友面前跟他吻别或说话。你多希望孩子能更成熟些。

孩子 18 岁时，你所记得的，是他们出生的那一天。从此之后，你和他（她）拥有了天长地久的爱。

当你在静静的房子里走来走去时，你纳闷他们去哪里了——你多希望孩子别这么快就长大了。

Growing Roots

When I was growing up, I had an old neighbor named Dr. Haggard. He didn't look like any doctor I'd ever known. He never yelled at us for playing in his yard. I remember him as someone who was a lot nicer than circumstances warranted.

When Dr. Haggard wasn't saving lives, he was planting trees. His house sat on ten acres, and his life's goal was to make it a forest.

The good doctor had some interesting theories concerning plant husbandry①. He came from the "No pain, no gain" school of horticulture. He never watered his new trees, which flew in the face of conventional wisdom. Once I asked why. He said that watering plants spoiled them, and that if you water them, each successive tree generation will grow weaker and weaker. So you have to make things rough for them and weed out the weenie[2] trees early on.

He talked about how watering trees made for shallow roots, and how trees that weren't watered had to grow deep roots in search of moisture. I took him to mean that deep roots were to be treasured.

So he never watered his trees. He'd plant an oak and, instead of watering it every morning, he'd beat it with a rolled-up newspaper. Smack! Slap! Pow! I asked him why he did that, and he said it was to get the tree's attention.

Dr. Haggard went to glory a couple of years after I left home. Every now and again, I walked by his house and looked at the trees that I'd watched him plant some twenty-five years ago. They're granite strong now. Big and robust. Those trees wake up in the morning and beat their chests and drink their black coffee.

I planted a couple of trees a few years back. Carried water to them for a solid summer. Sprayed them. Prayed over them. The whole nine yards. Two years of coddling has resulted in trees that expect to be waited on hand and foot. Whenever a cold wind blows in, they tremble and chatter their branches. Sissy trees.

Funny things about those trees of Dr. Haggard's. Adversity and deprivation seemed to benefit them in ways comfort and ease never could.

Every night before I go to bed, I check on my two sons. I stand over them and watch their little bodies, the rising and falling of life within. I often pray for them. Mostly I pray that their lives will be easy. But lately I've been thinking that it's time to change my prayer.

This change has to do with the inevitability of cold winds that hit us at the core. I know my children are going to encounter hardship, and I'm praying they won't be naive③. There are always hailstones hitting somewhere.

So I'm changing my prayer. Because life is tough, whether we want it to be or not. Too many times we pray for ease, but that's a prayer seldom met. What we need to do is pray for roots that reach deep into the Eternal, so when the rains fall and the winds blow, we won't be swept asunder④.

① husbandry　耕种;务农

② weenie　微小的,细小的

③ naive　幼稚的;轻信的;天真的

④ asunder　分离;化为碎片

植根

在我还是小孩子的时候，我有一个老邻居叫哈格德医生。他不像我所认识的其他任何一个医生。我们在他的院子里玩耍，他从不对我们大喊大叫。我记得他是一个非常和蔼的人。

哈格德医生不给人治病的时候就去种树。他的住所占地10 英亩，他的人生目标就是将它变成一片森林。

这个好医生对于如何耕作有一番有趣的理论。他坚信“不劳无获”的园艺种植理念。他从不浇灌他新种的树，这显然与常理相悖。有一次我问为什么，他说浇水会毁了这些树，如果浇水，每一棵成活的树的后代会变得越来越娇弱。所以你得把它们的生长环境变得艰苦些，尽早淘汰那些弱不禁风的树。

他还告诉我用水浇灌的树的根是如何的浅，而那些没有浇水的树的根必须钻入深深的泥土获得水分。我将他的话理解为：深根是十分宝贵的。

所以他从不给他的树浇水。他种了一棵橡树，每天早上，他不是给它浇水，而是用一张卷起的报纸抽打它。“啪！噼！砰！”我问他为什么这样做，他说是为了引起树的注意。

在我离家两年后，哈格德医生就去世了。我常常经过他的房子，看着那些25年前我曾看着他种下的那些树。如今它们已是像石头般硬朗了。枝繁叶茂、生气勃勃。这些树在早晨醒过来，拍打着胸脯，啜饮着苦难的汁水。

几年前我也种下两三棵树。整整一个夏天我都坚持为它们浇水。为它们喷杀虫剂，为它们祈祷。整整9平方码大的地方。两年的悉心呵护，结果两棵树弱不禁风。每当寒风吹起，它们就颤抖起来，枝叶直打战。娇里娇气的两棵树。

哈格德医生的树真是有趣。逆境和折磨带给它们的益处似乎是舒适和安逸永远无法给予的。

每天晚上睡觉前，我都要看看两个儿子。我俯视着他们那幼小的身体，生命就在其中起落沉浮。我总是为他们祈祷，总是祈祷他们的生活能一帆风顺。但后来我想该是改变我的祈祷词的时候了。

这改变是因为将吹在我们要害的不可避免的寒风。我知道我的孩子们总要遇到困难，我祈祷他们不会幼稚而脆弱。

在某些地方总会有寒风吹过。

所以我改变了我的祈祷词。因为不管我们愿不愿意，生活总是艰难的。我们已祈祷了太多的安逸，但却少有实现。我们所需要做的是祈祷深植我们的信念之根，这样我们就不会被雨打风吹所伤害。

On Motes and Beams

It is curious that our own offenses should seem so much less heinous[①] than the offenses of others. I suppose the reason is that we know all the circumstances that have occasioned them and so manage to excuse in ourselves what we cannot excuse in others. We turn our attention away from our own defects, and when we are forced by untoward events to consider them, find it easy to condone[②] them. For all I know we are right to do this; they are part of us and we must accept the good and bad in ourselves together.

But when we come to judge others, it is not by ourselves as we really are that we judge them, but by an image that we have formed of ourselves from which we have left out everything that offends our vanity or would discredit us in the eyes of the world. To take a trivial instance: how scornful we are when we catch someone out telling a lie; but who can say that he has never told not one, but a hundred?

There is not much to choose between men. They are all a hotchpotch[③] of greatness and littleness, of virtue and vice, of nobility and baseness. Some have more strength of character, or more opportunity, and so in one direction or another give their instincts freer play, but potentially they are the same. For my part, I do not think I am any better or any worse than most people, but I know that if I set down every action in my life and every thought that has crossed my mind, the world would consider me a monster of depravity[④]. The knowledge that these reveries are common to all men should inspire one with tolerance to oneself as well as to others. It is well also if they enable us to look upon our fellows, even the most eminent and respectable, with humor, and if they lead us to take ourselves not too seriously.

词汇

① heinous 可憎的,极恶的

② condone 宽恕

③ hotchpotch 杂烩

④ depravity 堕落

微尘与栋梁

让人奇怪的是，和别人的过错比起来，我们自身的过错往往不是那样的可恶。我想，其原因应该是我们知晓一切导致自己犯错的情况，因此能够设法谅解自己的错误，而别人的错误却不能谅解。我们对自己的缺点不甚关注，即便是深陷困境而不得不正视它们的时候，我们也会很容易就宽恕自己。据我所知，我们这样做是正确的。缺点是我们自身的一部分，我们必须接纳自己的好和坏。

但是当我们评判别人的时候，情况就不同了。我们不是通过真实的自我来评判别人，而是用一种自我形象来评判，这种自我形象完全摒弃了会伤害到自己的世俗的虚荣或者体面的东西。举一个小例子来说：当觉察到别人说谎时，我们是多么的蔑视他啊！但是，谁能够说自己从未说过谎？可能还不止100次呢。

人和人之间没什么大的差别。他们皆是伟大与渺小，善良与邪恶，高尚与低俗的混合体。有的人性格比较坚毅，或者机会比较多，因而在这个或那个方面，能够更自由地发挥自己的禀赋，但是人类的潜能却都是相同的。至于我自己，我认为自己并不比大多数人更好或者更差。但是我知道，假如我记下我生命中每一次举动和每一个掠过我脑海的想法的话，世界就会将我视为一个邪恶的怪物。每个人都会有这样的怪念头，这样的认识应当能够启发我们宽容自己，也宽容他人。假如因此我们得以用幽默的态度看待他人——即使那是天下最优秀最令人尊敬的人，假如我们因此不把自己看得过于重要的话，那是很有裨益的。

Go to School and Get Education

It is commonly believed in the United States that school is where people go to get an education. Nevertheless, it has been said that today children interrupt their education to go to school. The distinction① between schooling and education implied by this remark is important.

Education is much more open-ended and all-inclusive than schooling. Education knows no bounds. It can take place anywhere, whether in the shower or in the job, whether in a kitchen or on a tractor.

It includes both the formal learning that takes place at schools and the whole universe of informal learning. The agents of education can range from a revered grandparent to the people debating politics on the radio, from a child to a distinguished② scientist.

Whereas schooling has a certain predictability, education quite often produces surprises. A chance conversation with a stranger may lead a person to discover how little is known of other religions.

People are engaged in education from infancy on. Education, then, is a very broad, inclusive term. It is a lifelong process, a process that starts long before the start of school, and one that should be an integral part of one's entire life.

Schooling, on the other hand, is a specific, formalized[③] process, whose general pattern varies little from one setting to the next. Throughout a country, children arrive at school at approximately[④] the same time, take assigned seats, are taught by an adult, use similar textbooks, do homework, take exams, and so on.

The slices of reality that are to be learned, whether they are the alphabet or an understanding of the workings of government, have usually been limited by the boundaries of the subject being taught.

For example, high school students know that they are not likely to find out in their classes the truth about political problems in their communities or what the newest filmmakers are experimenting with.

There are definite conditions surrounding the formalized process of schooling.

词汇

① distinction 差别;区分;优秀

② distinguished 著名的,卓越的

③ formalized 形式化的

④ approximately 近似地

上学与受教育

在美国，人们通常认为上学是为了受教育。而现在却有人认为孩子们上学打断了他们受教育的过程。这种观念中的上学与受教育之间的区别非常重要。

与上学相比，教育更具开放性，内容更广泛。教育不受任何限制。它可以在任何场合下进行——在淋浴时，在工作时，在厨房里或拖拉机上。

它既包括在学校所受的正规教育，也包括一切非正规教育。传授知识的人可以是德高望重的老者，可以是收音机里进行政治辩论的人们，可以是小孩子，也可以是知名的科学家。

上学读书多少有点可预见性，而教育往往能带来意外的发现。与陌生人的一次随意谈话可能会使人认识到自己对其他宗教其实知之甚少。

人们从幼时起就开始受教育。因此，教育是一个内涵很丰富的词，它自始至终伴随人的一生，早在人们上学之前就开始了。教育应成为人生不可缺少的一部分。

然而，上学却是一个特定的形式化了的过程。在不同场合下，它的基本形式大同小异。在全国各地，孩子们几乎在同一时刻到达学校，坐在指定的座位上，由一位成年人传授知识，使用大致相同的教材，做作业，考试等等。

他们所学的现实生活中的一些片断，如字母表或政府的运作，往往受到科目范围的限制。

例如，高中生们知道，在课堂上他们没法弄清楚他们社区里政治问题的真情，也不会了解到最新潮的电影制片人在做哪些尝试。

学校教育这一格式化的过程是有特定限制的。

Things You Need to Know When You Are Young

1. Most of it doesn't matter. So much of what I got excited about, anxious about, or wasted my time and energy on, turned out not to matter. There are only a few things that truly count for a happy life. I wish I had known to concentrate on those and ignore the rest.

2. Waiting to do something until you can be sure of doing it exactly right means waiting for ever. One of the greatest adventures anyone can have is the willingness to make a fool of themselves publicly and often. There's no better way to learn and develop.

3. Following the latest fashion is spiritual and intellectual suicide. You can be a cheap imitation of the idea of the moment; or you can be a unique individual. The choice is yours. Religion isn't the opiate① of the masses, fashion is.

4. If you make your work your life, you're making your life into hard work. Like most people, I confused myself by looking at people like artists and musicians whose life's "work" fills their time. That isn't work. It's just who they are.

5. The quickest and simplest way to wreck any relationship is to listen to gossip. The worst way to spend your time is spreading more. People who spread gossip are the plague-carriers of our day. Cockroaches are clean, kindly creatures in comparison.

6. Every winner is destined to be a loser in due course. It's great to be up on the winner's podium. Just don't imagine you can stay there for ever. Worst of all is being determined to do so, by any means available.

7. You can rarely, if ever, please, placate, change, or modify an asshole. The best thing you can do is stay away from every one you encounter. Being an asshole is a contagious disease. The more time you spend around one, the more likely you are to catch it and become one too.

8. Everything takes twice as long as you plan for and produces results about half as good as you hoped. There's no reason to be downhearted about this. Just allow for it and move on.

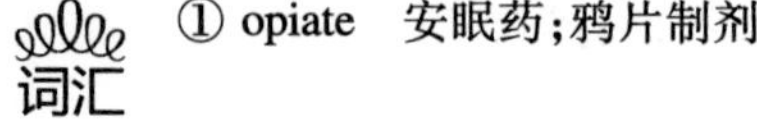

① opiate　安眠药;鸦片制剂

年轻时一定要知道的事

1. 拥有一颗平常心。有太多事情曾让我为其兴奋，为其焦虑，抑或是浪费了我的时间以及精力，到最后却被证明是无关紧要的。只有少数一些事情与幸福生活有关。我多么希望早点知道这些，以便能把精力都投入到那些关乎幸福的事，而不是其他。

2. 等待有把握时再去做一件事，往往意味着永远的等待。一个人能做的最大的冒险的事情，就是乐意经常在公共场合暴露自己的愚昧。没有什么能比这样学得更快。

3. 盲目追赶潮流是对精神和智力的扼杀。你可以成为一个廉价的时尚木偶，也可以成为独一无二的你，这些都在于自己的选择。信仰不是群众的鸦片，流行才是。

4. 如果你将工作等同于生活，那么你将为工作而生活。

和很多人一样，当看到那些艺术家和音乐家的工作几乎是他们的全部生活时，我感到很困惑。其实那不是工作，那是他们的自我。

5. 破坏关系最快最简单的方法就是听信谣言。浪费时间的最糟糕方式是传播这些谣言。传播流言蜚语的人好比瘟疫的携带者，相比之下，蟑螂都比他们干净、善良。

6. 没有永久的胜利者。踏上冠军宝座是件好事情。但不要梦想着可以永久占据这个位置，最糟糕的是，你正决定为达此目的而不择手段。

7. 不可能取悦、安抚或改造一个混蛋。你能做的最好方式，是对他们敬而远之。变成混蛋也能传染，你和他们待的时间越长，你也越有可能染上混蛋的习气而成为混蛋。

8. 任何事情都是花掉你计划的两倍时间，最后却只换来你一半的期望结果。没什么好为此沮丧的，让它去吧，你要继续前行。

Please Dress Me in Red

In my dual[①] profession as an educator and health care provider, I have worked with numerous children infected with the virus that causes AIDS[②]. The relationships that I have had with these special kids have been gifts in my life. They have taught me so many things, but I have especially learned that great courage can be found in the smallest of packages. Let me tell you about Tim.

Tim was born infected with HIV; his mother was also infected. From the very beginning of his life, he was dependent on medications to enable him to survive. When he was six, he had a tube surgically inserted in a vein in his chest. This tube was connected to a pump, which he carried in a small backpack on his back. Medications were hooked up to this pump and were continuously supplied through this tube to his bloodstream. At times, he also needed supplemented oxygen to support his breathing.

Tim wasn't willing to give up one single moment of his childhood to this deadly disease. It was not unusual to find him playing and racing around his backyard, wearing his medicine-laden backpack and dragging his tank of oxygen behind him in his little wagon. All of us who knew Tim marveled at his pure joy in being alive and the energy it gave him. Tim's mom often teased him by telling him that he moved so fast she needed to dress him in red. That way, when she peered through the window to check on him playing in the yard, she could quickly spot him.

This dreaded disease eventually wore down even the likes of a little dynamo③ like Tim. He grew quite ill and, unfortunately, so did his HIV-infected mother. When it became apparent that he wasn't going to survive, Tim's mom talked to him about death. She comforted him by telling Tim that she was dying too, and that she would be with him soon in heaven.

A few days before his death, Tim beckoned me over to his hospital bed and whispered, "I might die soon. I'm not scared. When I die, please dress me in red. Mom promised she's coming to heaven, too. I'll be playing when she gets there, and I want to make sure she can find me."

词汇

① dual 双重的

② AIDS (Acquired Immure Deficiency Syndrome) 艾滋病

③ dynamo 发电机;精力充沛的人

请给我穿上红色衣服

作为一名教育和保健护理工作者，我曾经和无数感染上艾滋病病毒的孩子打过交道。我和这些特殊的孩子之间的关系是生活赋予我的礼物。他们教会我许多东西，尤其让我懂得了即使在最弱小的人物身上也能发现其所蕴涵的巨大勇气。让我告诉你蒂姆的故事。

蒂姆出生前就从母体感染上艾滋病病毒。自他来到人间就一直靠药物维持生命。他 6 岁时做手术，胸部插了一根管子，管子连着他背的背包里的泵。泵不断地把药通过管子输入他的血液。有时他还需要补充氧气帮助呼吸。

蒂姆不愿把童年的一分一秒屈服于致命的疾病。经常能发现他背着装药的背包和拖着载有氧气罐的小车在他家后院玩耍奔跑。我们所有认识蒂姆的人都惊叹生命带给他那纯朴的欢乐和赋予他的活力。蒂姆的妈妈经常逗他说，他跑得那么快，得给他穿件红衣服。这样，她透过窗户查看他在院子里玩得怎样时，能一眼发现他。

可怕的疾病最终还是拖垮了精力充沛得像台小电动机似的蒂姆。他的病情越来越严重，不幸的是，身染艾滋病病毒的妈妈也病入膏肓。蒂姆即将撒手人寰时，妈妈和他谈起死亡。她安慰他说，她也将要离开人世，不久会和他在天堂见面。

蒂姆病逝前几天，招呼我到他病床前，低声对我说："我可能就要死了，我不害怕。我死时，请给我穿上红色的衣服。妈妈答应我她也会来天堂的。她来的时候我会在玩，我得保证她能找到我。"

4 Classes May Lead You to Wealth

Economics

If you understand how the economy got to the point where it is today, it helps you identify where your money should be. You can pick out the right investments① and turn away from the bad ones. You can identify which direction your business should go in, including whether to take advantage of certain trends or cut out excess inventory②.

Finance

Finance helps you understand how the time value of money works and how various investment vehicles operate. One of the keys to becoming rich is comprehending③ how money works when it's not in your hands. A finance course (preferably one geared towards entrepreneurship) will teach you what you need to reach this level of understanding. There might be some math involved, but it won't bother you. It'll just make you a stronger and savvier[4] investor.

Any History Course

History can be boring. But if you look at history from a different viewpoint, it can open doors for you. The most valuable aspect of history is its ability to convey to us the mistakes of others. Studying history helps you learn from others so that, hopefully, you won't commit the same mistakes.

Writing and Composition

Succeeding as an entrepreneur requires that you should be able to express yourself and your ideas. Whether it involves pitching an idea to an investor, writing a press release, or composing a business plan, entrepreneurs need to communicate. More often than not, this communication is done in writing. Basic composition and grammar skills can do wonders for your ability to convey your ideas and your mindset.

① investment 投资

② inventory 详细目录;存货清单

③ comprehend 理解,领会

④ savvy 理解能力;机智;悟性

大学可能会让你致富的四门课程

经济学

对经济发展态势的了解会让你看清投资的方向。你就可以避免错误投资并找到正确的投资领域。此外，你还能清楚地了解今后自己业务发展的方向，例如是否有必要利用当前的某种趋势，或是大幅削减超额的存货清单。

金融学

金融学会帮你理解金钱的时间价值以及不同投资工具的运作方式。要想发财，关键之一就是要了解当钱不在你手上的时候它们是如何运作的。一门关于金融的（最好是针对于如何管理企业的）课程会教你怎样达到那样的理解层次。或许这会涉及数学，但还是难不倒你的。相反地，它会让你成为一个更强更有悟性的投资者。

任意一门历史课

历史可能会很枯燥。但是如果你能从一个新的角度去看待它，你就会得到很多启示。你能从历史中看到他人所犯的错误，这是它最有价值的地方。学习历史，能够让你避免再犯前人所犯的错误。

写作

要想成为一名成功的企业家，你必须具有表达观点以及展示自我的能力。因为无论是要向投资者表述一个构思，写记者会文稿，还是拟定一份商业计划书，你都需要与别人沟通。大多数情况下，这种沟通都是通过书面形式完成的。当你传达自己的观点和想法时，对基本的写作以及语法技巧的掌握就能让你事半功倍。

Girls of Summer

We lived on the banks of the Tennessee River, and we owned the summers when we were girls. We ran wild through humid summer days that never ended but only melted one into the other. We floated down rivers of weekdays with no school, no rules, no parents, and no constructs other than our fantasies. We were good girls, my sister and I. We had nothing to rebel against. This was just life as we knew it, and we knew the summers to be long and to be ours.

I liked walking to the mailbox in my bare feet and leaving footprints on the dewy[①] grass. I imagined that feeling the wetness on the bottom of my feet made me a poet. I had never read poetry, outside of some Emily Dickinson. But I imagined that people who knew of such things would walk to their mailboxes through the morning dew in their bare feet.

We planned our weddings with the help of Barbie dolls and the tiny purple wildflowers growing in our side yard. We became scientists and tested concoctions of milk, orange juice and cola. We ate handfuls of bittersweet chocolate chips and licked peanut butter off spoons. When we ran out of cheese to eat, we snitched sugary Flintstones vitamins out of the medicine cabinet. We became masters of the Kraft macaroni② and cheese lunch, and we dutifully called our mother at work three times a day to give her updates on our adventures. But don't call too often or speak too loudly or whine too much, we told ourselves, or else they'll get annoyed and she'll get fired and the summers will get ruined.

词汇

① dewy　带露水的

② macaroni　通心粉

夏日女孩

还是小女孩的时候，夏天是我们的，那时，我家住在田纳西河畔。在那些永无尽头、一天天彼此交融的湿润夏日里，我们撒了野地跑着。我们在长长的周日中放任自己，没有学校的管束，没有规则的羁绊，没有父母的训诫，没有既定的观念，只有属于我们自己的梦幻。我和姐姐，我们都是好女孩，没有什么需要我们去对抗和反叛的。这就是我们所知的生活，我们知道夏日正长，而且是属于我们的。

我喜欢赤足走向我家的信箱，在沾着露水的草地上留下脚印。我想象着，足底湿漉漉的感觉使我成了一个诗人。除了艾米莉·狄金森的一些作品外，我其实从不读诗。但是我想，懂得这类东西的人一定会赤足踏着晨露走向他们的信箱。

我们用芭比娃娃和旁边小花园里紫色的小野花来筹办我

们的婚礼游戏。我们是科学家，尝试牛奶、橙汁和可乐的混合物。我们吃光一把又一把甜中带苦的巧克力片，把勺子上的花生酱舔得干干净净。奶酪吃完了，我们就从药箱里偷拿有甜味的弗林斯通复合维生素片。我们成了用卡夫通心面和干酪烹制午餐的专家，并尽职尽责地每天给正在上班的妈妈打3个电话汇报我们的最新情况。但是，我们告诫自己：不要打太多电话，不要说得太大声，也不要在电话里过多地诉苦，要不然他们就会生气，妈妈就会被解雇，美好的夏日也就被毁了。

Learning from a Tough Teacher

Sooner or later everyone gets a teacher. He does not like you—or whom you seem not to like. Last year's teacher would have given you an A. This year's teacher tells you to work harder. You probably badmouth① him under your breath. But you may also stretch for a higher level of achievement. You may earn that A—and learn a lot in the process.

Of course, this year's tough teacher may not be a stimulating fireball② but a drone③ who doesn't recognize a good student when he's staring at one. This happens. In real life as well, there are tiresome landlords, unfair bosses, drippy④ colleagues. If what you wind up learning from a tough teacher isn't how to study harder, but how to make the best of a less-than-ideal situation, that, too, is educational.

词汇

① badmouth　说某人坏话

② fireball　火球

③ drone　雄蜂；懒惰者

④ drippy　软弱无用的；过于伤感的

求学从严

每个人迟早会碰到一位老师，他不喜欢你，或者你不喜欢他。上一年度的老师给你的成绩是A，本年度的老师却要求你更刻苦地学习。你也许对他耿耿于怀，但你仍然努力获得更好的成绩，你得了A，整个过程中你获益匪浅。

当然，本年度凶巴巴的老师也许不是一个催人奋进的、工作起来劲头十足的人，而是一个有眼无珠、不识真才的怠工者。这种情况随处可见。现实生活中有着令人讨厌的房东、不公道的老板和拖泥带水的同事。如果你最终从严师那儿学到的不是如何刻苦学习，而是如何变不利为有利，那也受益匪浅。

Grandfather's Expectation

We tried so hard to make things better for our kids that we made them worse. For my grandchildren, I'd know better.

I'd really like for them to know about hand-me-down clothes and home-made ice cream and leftover meat loaf. I really would.

My cherished grandson, I hope you learn humility① by surviving failure and that you learn to be honest even when no one is overlooking.

If you want a slingshot, I hope your father teaches you how to make one instead of buying one. I hope you learn to dig in the dirt and read books, and when you learn to use computers, you also learn how to add and subtract② in your head.

I hope you get razzed by friends when you have your first

crush[3] on a girl, and that when you talk back to your mother you learn what Ivory soap tastes like.

May you skin your knee climbing a mountain, burn your hand on the stove and stick your tongue on a frozen flagpole.

I hope you get sick when someone blows smoke in your face. I don't care if you try beer once, but I hope you won't like it. And if a friend offers you a joint or any drugs, I hope you are smart enough to realize that person is not your friend.

I sure hope you make time to sit on a porch with your grandma or go fishing with your uncle.

I hope your mother punishes you when you throw a baseball through a neighbor's window, and that she hugs you and kisses you when you give her a plaster[4] of pared mold of your hand.

These things I wish for you—tough times and disappointment, hard work and happiness.

① humility 谦逊，谦恭

② subtract 减(去)

③ crush 对(某人的)强烈而短暂的喜爱，迷恋

④ plaster 石膏

爷爷的期望

我们竭尽全力想让我们的子女们过得更好，结果却是适得其反。对我的孙辈们，我就明智得多了。

我真的希望他们能够了解什么是传下来的旧衣服，自制的冰淇淋，以及吃剩的肉糜卷。我真的这样希望。

我的宝贝孙子，我希望你在经受失败的考验之后能学会谦卑，也希望你能学会诚实——即使在没有人监督你的时候。

如果你想要一把弹弓，我希望你父亲能教你怎样自己做一把，而不是为你买一把现成的。我还希望你能学会挖泥巴和读书；而当你学会使用电脑时，你也应该学会加减法的心算。

当你第一次恋上一个女孩时，我希望你会受到朋友们的嘲弄；而当你跟你母亲顶嘴时，希望她叫你尝一尝象牙肥皂的滋味。

但愿你能在爬山时弄破膝盖上的皮，或者在炉子上烧伤手，或者让舌头粘在结冰的旗杆上。

我希望吸烟者对着你的脸上喷吐烟雾时，你会感到恶心。如果你尝试喝一次啤酒，我不会在意；但是我希望你不要喜欢上它。如果有一位朋友请你吸一口含大麻的香烟，或者任何毒品，我希望你明智地意识到他不会是你的朋友。

我当然希望你能抽时间来陪你奶奶在门廊上坐一坐，或者陪你叔叔钓钓鱼。

如果你把棒球扔进了邻居的窗户，我希望你母亲惩罚你。如果你能剪掉指甲，用石膏做一只自己的手的模型送给你妈妈，我希望她会给你拥抱和亲吻。

我希望你能经历：艰难困苦和伤心失望，辛勤工作和幸福生活。

We Never Told Him He Couldn't Do It.

My son Joey was born with clubfeet. The doctors assured[①] us that with treatment he would be able to walk normally but would never run very well. The first three years of his life were spent in surgery[②], casts and braces. By the time he was eight, you wouldn't know he had a problem when you saw him walk.

The children in our neighborhood ran around as most children do during play, and Joey would jump right in and run and paly, too. We never told him that he probably wouldn't be able to run as well as the other children. So he didn't know.

In the seventh grade he decided to go out for the cross-country team. Every day he trained with the team. He worked harder and ran more than any of the others—perhaps he sensed[③] that the abilities that seemed to come naturally to so many others did not come naturally to him. Although the entire team runs, only the top seven runners have the potential[④] to score points for the school. We didn't tell him he probably would never make the team, so he didn't know.

He continued to run four to five miles a day, every day—even the day he had a 103-degree Fahrenheit fever. I was worried, so I went to look for him after school. I found him running all alone. I asked him how he felt. "Okay," he said. He had two more miles to go. The sweat ran down his face and his eyes were glassy[⑤] from his fever. Yet he looked straight ahead and kept running. We never told him he couldn't run for miles with a 103-degree Fahrenheit fever. So he didn't know.

Two weeks later, the names of the team runners were called. Joey was number six on the list. Joey had made the team. He was in the seventh grade—the other six team members were all eighth graders. We never told him he shouldn't expect to make the team. We never told him he couldn't do it. We never told him he couldn't do it … so he didn't know. He just did it.

词汇

① assure　确保

② surgery　外科；手术室

③ sense　感觉，了解

④ potential　潜在的，可能的

⑤ glassy　眼睛无神的

我们从不说他做不到

我的儿子琼尼降生时，他的双脚向上弯着，医生向我们保证说经过治疗，小琼尼可以像常人一样走路，但像常人一样跑步的可能性则微乎其微。琼尼三岁之前一直在接受治疗，和支架、石膏模子打交道。到他八岁的时候，他走路的样子已让人看不出他的脚有过毛病。

邻居的小孩子们做游戏的时候总是跑过来跑过去。毫无疑问小琼尼看到他们玩就会马上加进去跑啊闹的。我们从不告诉他不能像别的孩子那样跑，我们从不说他和别的孩子不一样。所以他不知道。

七年级的时候，琼尼决定参加跑步横穿全美的比赛。每天他和大伙一块儿训练。也许是意识到自己先天不如别人，他训练得比任何人都刻苦。训练队的前七名选手可以参加最后比赛，为学校拿分。我们没有告诉琼尼也许他根本不会成为前七名，所以他不知道。

他坚持每天跑 4 ~ 5 英里。我永远不会忘记有一次，他发高烧到 103 华氏度，但仍坚持训练。我为他担心，于是去学校看他，发现他正在一个人跑步呢。我问他感觉怎么样，“很好。”他说。还剩下最后两英里。他满脸是汗，眼睛因为发烧失去了光彩。然而他目不斜视，坚持着跑下来。我们从没有告诉他他不能发着高烧去跑 4 英里的路，所以他不知道。

两个星期后，在决赛前 3 天，长跑队的名次被确定下来。琼尼是第六名，他成功了。他才是个七年级学生，而其余的人都是八年级学生。我们从没有告诉他不要去期望入选，我们从没有对他说他不会成功。是的，从没说起过……所以他不知道，但他却做到了！

Bumps and Bruises

"Life is full of bumps and bruises[①]. It's what you learn from it and what you do with it that makes you who you are."

I was reading this article in *Glamour* magazine and it was about these five women who overcame deadly situations and got on with their lives. These women went through a double lung transplant, an open heart surgery and then gave birth to[②] twins, a cancer survivor[③], a deadly bacterial[④] infection, and one of the women, who was still a teenager, survived knife wounds that most people wouldn't survive.

This article got me thinking about how people go about their lives. Life is not a smooth ride. Some people, when they hit a bump, give up and turn around while others find ways to go over the bump or around the bump. I believe that everyone should do the latter[⑤] and be like these five women and find ways to get around these bumps.

So when you reach a bump on the road called life, don't give up because you're not the only person to ever reach that particular bump and you're not the last. Be an example for your followers!

词汇

① bruise 撞伤,擦伤

② give birth to 生(孩子)

③ survivor 生还者

④ bacterial 细菌的

⑤ latter 后面的,后者的

人生礁石

“人的一生难免磕磕绊绊，正是这些艰难让你学会成长，学会面对，成为今日之栋梁。”

我曾在《魅力》这本杂志上读到这样一篇文章：文章讲述五个女人如何度过她们生命的危难时刻，继续行走在她们的生命之路上。她们之中有的经历过双肺移植手术；有的做过一次心脏手术，然后还生了一对双胞胎；有的是癌症魔爪下的生还者；有的被致命的细菌感染过；还有一个女人，在青少年时遭受了极其严重的刀伤，大多数人都过不了这个坎，而她过了。

这篇文章不禁让我对人们应对人生的态度有了一番思索。人生的航程并不是一帆风顺的，有些人触了礁便放弃了，转头回去；而有些人则千方百计寻路绕过这些礁石。我想，每个人都应该像后者一样，学习那五个女人，绕过生命中的礁石。

所以当你在人生之途上遇到暗礁，不要放弃，因为你不是唯一一个，也不是最后一个触礁的人。为后来者树立一个良好的榜样吧！

Golden Goals

I will set goals for the day, the week, the month, the year, and my life. Just as the rain must fall before the wheat will crack① its shell and sprout, so must I have objectives before my life will crystallize②. In setting my goals I will consider my best performance of the past and multiply③ it a hundredfold. This will be the standard by which I will live in the future. Never will I be of concern that my goals are too high for is it not better to aim my spear at the moon and strike only an eagle than to arm my spear at the eagle and strike only a rock?

The height of my goals will not hold me in awe though I may stumble④ often before they are reached. If I stumble I will rise and my falls will not concern me for all men must stumble often to reach the hearth. Only a worm is free from the worry of stumbling. I am not a worm. I am not an onion plant. I am not a sheep. I am a man. Let others build a cave with their clay[5]. I will build a castle with mine.

I will commit[6] not the terrible crime of aiming too low. I will do the work that a failure will not do. I will always let my reach exceed my grasp. I will never be content with my performance in the market. I will always raise my goals as soon as they are attained. I will always strive to make the next hour better than this one. I will always announce[7] my goals to the world.

词汇

① crack　裂缝

② crystallize　明确

③ multiply　增加;繁衍

④ stumble　使困惑,使遭受挫折

⑤ clay　黏土,泥土

⑥ commit　犯(错误),干(坏事)

⑦ announce　宣布,通告

远大的目标

我要为每一天、每个星期、每个月、每一年、甚至我的一生确立目标。正像小麦种子需要雨水的滋润才能破土而出、发芽长叶一样，我的生命也须有目的方能结出硕果。在制定目标的时候，不妨参考过去最好的成绩，使其发扬光大。这必须成为我未来生活的准则。永远不要担心目标过高。取法其上，得乎其中，取法其中，得乎其下。

高远的目标不会让我望而生畏，虽然在达到目标以前我可能屡受挫折。摔倒了，再爬起来，我不灰心，因为每个人在抵达目标之前都会受到挫折。只有小爬虫不必担心摔倒。我不是小爬虫，不是洋葱，不是绵羊。我是一个人。让别人用黏土造穴吧，我要建一座城堡。

我不能放低目标。我要做失败者不愿做的事。我不停留在力所能及的事上。我不满足于现有的成就。目标达到后，再定一个更高的目标。我要努力使下一刻比此刻更好。我要常常向世人宣告我的目标。

A Lesson of Life

"Everything happens for the best," my mother said whenever I faced disappointment. "If you carry on, one day something good will happen. And you'll realized that it wouldn't have happened if not for that previous disappointment."

Mother was right, as I discovered after graduating from college in 1932, I had decided to try for a job in radio, then work my way up to sports announcer. I hitchhiked① to Chicago and knocked on the door of every station—and got turned down every time.

In one studio, a kind lady told me that big stations couldn't risk hiring an inexperienced person. "Go out in the sticks and find a small station that'll give you a chance," she said.

I thumbed[②] home to Dixon, Illinois.

While there were no radio-announcing jobs in Dixon, my father said Montgomery Ward had opened a store and wanted a local athlete[③] to manage its sports department. Since Dixon was where I had played high school football, I applied. The job sounded just right for me. But I wan't hired.

My disappointment must have shown. "Everything happens for the best," Mom reminded me. Dad offered me the car to hunt job. I tried WOC Radio in Davenport, Iowa. The program director, a wonderful Scotsman named Peter MacArthur told me they had already hired an announcer[④].

As I left his office, my frustration boiled over. I asked aloud, "How can a fellow get to be a sports announcer if he can't get a job in a radio station?" I was waiting for the elevator when I heard MacArthur calling, "What was you said about sports? Do you know anything about football?" Then he stood me before a microphone and asked me broadcast an imaginary game. And Peter told me I would be broadcasting Saturday's game!

On my way home, as I have many times since, I thought of my mother's words: "If you carry on, one day something good will happen. Something wouldn't have happened if not for that previous[⑤] disappointment."

I often wonder what direction my life might have taken if I'd not gotten the job at Montgomery Ward.

词汇

① hitchhike　搭便车

② thumb　示意要求搭车

③ athlete　运动员

④ announcer　广播员

⑤ previous　以前的

生活的一课

“一切都会好的。”每当我遇到挫折的时候，母亲总会这样说，“如果你坚持住，总有一天会有好事发生。那时你会意识到，如果没有先前的挫折，好运也不会降临。”

母亲说得对，当我 1932 年从大学毕业之后，我发现了这一点。当时，我决心在电台找一份工作，然后逐步走上当一名体育解说员之路。我搭便车来到芝加哥，敲响了每一家电台的大门——但每一次都遭到拒绝。

在一家电台，一位好心的女士告诉我，大电台不会冒险雇佣没有经验的新人。“打起精神来，去找一家愿意给你机会的小电台试试。”她说。

于是我搭车回到家乡伊利诺伊州的迪克森。

然而，在迪克森没有电台解说员的工作，父亲说蒙哥马利·沃德区新开了一家商店，想雇佣一位当地的运动员管理体育部。因为我在高中时曾在迪克森踢过足球，于是我递交了一份申请表，这个工作听起来正适合我。然而，我没有被录用。

我的失望写在了脸上。“一切都会好的。”母亲提醒我说。父亲给我提供一辆车，让我去找工作。在爱荷华州的达文波特市，我去 WOC 电台碰运气。电台节目部主任是一个优秀的苏格兰人，名字叫彼得·麦克阿瑟，他告诉我说他们已经聘用了一个播音员。

离开他的办公室，我的挫折感升到了极点，我大声问自己：“如果不能在电台找到一份工作，如何能够走上体育解说员之路？”当我等电梯的时候，我听到了麦克阿瑟的喊声：“你说什么体育？你懂足球吗？”然后，他让我站在麦克风前，让我解说一场假想的比赛。然后麦克阿瑟告诉我，我将解说星期六的比赛！

在回家的路上，就像以往许多次一样，我想到了母亲的话：“如果你坚持住，总有一天会有好事发生。那时你会意识到，如果没有先前的失望，好运也不会降临。”

我常常思索，如果我没有在蒙哥马利·沃德区得到那份工作，我的生活将会怎样。

Bad Temper

There once was a little boy who had a bad temper. His father gave him a bag of nails and told him that every time he lost his temper, he must hammer[1] a nail into the fence. The first day the boy had driven 37 nails into the fence. Over the next few weeks, as he learned to control his anger, the number of nails hammered daily gradually[2] dwindled down[3]. He discovered it was easier to hold his temper than to drive those nails into the fence.

Finally the day came when the boy didn't lose his temper at all. He told his father about it and the father suggested that the boy now pull out one nail for each day that he was able to hold his temper. The day passed and the young boy was finally able to tell his father that all the nails were gone. The father took his son by the hand and led him to the fence. He said,

"You have done well, my son, but look at the holes in those fences. The fence will never be the same. When you say things in anger, they leave a scar[④] just like this one. You can put a knife in a man and draw it out. It won't matter how many times you say I'm sorry, the wound is still there."

词汇

① hammer 锤击,敲打

② gradually 逐步地,渐渐地

③ dwindle down 逐渐减少

④ scar 伤痕

坏脾气

从前，有一个小男孩脾气很坏。他的父亲给了他一包钉子，告诉他每次发脾气的时候，必须把一根钉子钉进篱笆里。第一天，这个男孩把37根钉子钉进了篱笆。在以后的几个星期里，他渐渐学会了如何控制自己的怒气，这样每天锤进篱笆的钉子的数目也越来越少。他发现，控制自己的脾气比把那些钉子钉进篱笆更容易。

终于有一天，这个孩子再也不发脾气了。他把这件事告诉了他的父亲。父亲对这个男孩建议道，如果他能控制自己的脾气，一天就可以拔掉一根钉子。日子一天天过去了，最后这个男孩告诉他的父亲，所有的钉子都被拔下来了。父亲牵着儿子的手把他领到篱笆旁，说道："你做得很好，我的孩子，但是你看这篱笆上的洞。这些篱笆永远不会跟从前一样了。当你带着怒气讲话的时候，你给别人造成的创伤正如这些洞一样。这就像你拿着刀子刺伤了别人又把刀子拔出来一样。无论你说多少次‘对不起’，都无济于事，伤疤依然如故。”

Catch of a Lifetime

He was 11 years old and went fishing every chance he got from the dock at his family's cabin on an island in the middle of a New Hampshire lake.

On the day before the bass season opened, he and his father were fishing early in the evening, catching sunfish and perch with worms. Then he tied on a small silver lure and practiced casting. The lure struck the water and caused colored ripples in the sunset, then silver ripples as the moon rose over the lake.

When his fishing rod doubled over, he knew something huge was on the other end. His father watched with admiration as the boy skillfully worked the fish alongside the dock.

Finally, he very gingerly[①] lifted the exhausted fish from the water. It was the largest one he had ever seen, but it was a bass.

The boy and his father looked at the handsome fish, gills playing back and forth[②] in the moonlight. The father lit a match and looked at his watch. It was 10 p. m. —two hours before the season opened. He looked at the fish, then at the boy.

"You'll have to put it back, son," he said.

"Dad!" cried the boy.

"There will be other fish," said his father.

"Not as big as this one," cried the boy.

He looked around the lake. No other fishermen or boats were anywhere around in the moonlight. He looked again at his father. Even though no one had seen them, nor could anyone ever know what time he caught the fish, the boy could tell by the clarity[③] of his father's voice that the decision was not negotiable[④]. He slowly worked the hook out of the lip of the huge bass and lowered it into the black water.

The creature swished its powerful body and disappeared. The boy suspected[⑤] that he would never again see such a great fish.

That was 34 years ago. Today, the boy is a successful architect in New York City. His father's cabin is still there on the island in the middle of the lake. He takes his own son and daughters fishing from the same dock.

And he was right. He has never again caught such a magnificent[⑥] fish as the one he landed that night long ago. But he does see that same fish again and again—every time he comes up against a question of ethics.

For, as his father taught him, ethics are simple matters of right and wrong. It is only the practice of ethics that is difficult. Do we do right when no one is looking? Do we refuse to cut corners to get the design in on time? Or refuse to trade stocks based on information that we know we aren't supposed to have?

We would if we were taught to put the fish back when we were young. For we would have learned the truth. The decision to do right lives fresh and fragrant in our memory. It is a story we will proudly tell our friends and grandchildren. Not about how we had a chance to beat the system and took it, but about how we did the right thing and were forever strengthened.

词汇

① gingerly 极度小心地,谨慎地

② back and forth 来回地,反复地

③ clarity 清楚;透明

④ negotiable 可通行的;可协商的

⑤ suspect 怀疑;猜想

⑥ magnificent 极好的

一生的收获

在 11 岁那年，他一有机会就会到位于新罕布什尔州湖心岛上他家小屋旁的码头上钓鱼。

在鲈鱼季节开放的前一天，他和父亲在傍晚早早就开始垂钓。他们用小虫做诱饵来钓太阳鱼和鲈鱼。他在银色的鱼钩上放好诱饵，开始练习抛线。鱼钩撞到水面上，在夕阳中漾起一片金光闪闪的涟漪。接着，当月亮升起来时，涟漪就变得银光闪闪了。

当他的鱼竿弯下去的时候，他知道线的那一端一定是钓到了一条大鱼。他灵巧地在码头边沿和那条鱼周旋。父亲用充满赞赏的眼神关注着他。

最后，他很小心地将那条筋疲力尽的鱼从水里拉了出来。这可是他所见过的最大的一条鱼，而且还是一条鲈鱼。

男孩和他的父亲凝视着这条漂亮的鱼，它的鱼鳃在月光下一张一翕。父亲点燃一根火柴，看了一下表。现在是10点——离鲈鱼季节的开禁时间还有两个小时。他看了看鱼，又看了看那个男孩。

“你要把它再放回去，儿子。”他说。

“爸爸！”男孩喊道。

“还会有其他鱼的。”父亲说。

“但肯定不会像这条一样大。”男孩喊道。

他看了看湖的周围。在月光的笼罩下，周围没有其他的渔民或船只。他再一次看着父亲。尽管并没有人看着他们，也没有人知道他们是什么时候钓到鱼的，但从父亲那坚定的语气中，男孩知道这个决定是不可更改的。他慢慢地将渔钩从大鲈鱼的唇上拿下来，然后蹲下来把那条鱼再放回水里。

那条鱼摆了摆它强健的躯体，消失在水里。男孩想他再也不可能看到那么大的鱼了。

那件事已经过去34年了。而今，那个男孩已经成为纽约城里一个成功的建筑师。他父亲的小屋仍然矗立于湖心岛上。他带着自己的儿子和女儿回到同一个码头去钓鱼。

他当时的猜想是对的。他再也没有见过那么大的鱼了，但是，在他每次面对道德难题时，那条大鱼总会浮现在他的眼前。

因为正如父亲告诉他的那样，道德就是简单的对和错的问题，但困难的是付诸行动。在没人旁观时，我们能否仍然做得对？为了将图纸及时送到，我们是否会抄近路？或者在掌握了不该知道的消息后是否拒绝进行股票交易。

当我们年轻的时候，如果有人要让我们把鱼放回去，我们应该去做，因为我们将从中学到真理。选择去做正确事情的决定将在我们的记忆里历久弥新。我们可以把这个故事自豪地讲给我们的朋友和后辈听。这并不是关于如何攻击某种体制并战胜它，而是关于如何去做正确的事情，从而变得坚强。

图书在版编目(CIP)数据

夏日女孩:英汉对照/浩瀚编.—厦门:厦门大学出版社,2011.11

(午后时光休闲阅读系列之成长笔记)

ISBN 978-7-5615-4042-8

Ⅰ.①夏… Ⅱ.①浩… Ⅲ.①英语-汉语-对照读物②散文集-世界 Ⅳ.①H319.4:I

中国版本图书馆 CIP 数据核字(2011)第 202650 号

厦门大学出版社出版发行

(地址:厦门市软件园二期望海路 39 号 邮编:361008)

http://www.xmupress.com

xmup @ public.xm.fj.cn

厦门市明亮彩印有限公司印刷

2011 年 11 月第 1 版 2011 年 11 月第 1 次印刷

开本:889×1194 1/32 印张:2.5

字数:40 千字 印数:1～3 000 册

定价:14.00 元